AWESOME JOKES

8 THAT EVERY YEAR OLD SHOULD KNOW!

Joke research: Olivera Ristovska

Design: Fanni Williams / thehappycolourstudio.com
Icons made by: Freepik from www.flaticon.com

www.matwaugh.co.uk

Produced by Big Red Button Books,
a division of Say So Media Ltd.

ISBN: 978-1-9999147-4-5

Published: March 2018
This edition: July 2019

AWESOME JOKES

8

THAT EVERY YEAR OLD SHOULD KNOW!

MAT WAUGH

ILLUSTRATIONS BY INDREK SILVER EINBERG

Introduction

What makes you laugh?

I saw a video of a dog on a skateboard. That made me chuckle.

My brother once lost his welly in the mud. That made me laugh out loud.

My friend once told me a joke that was so funny, it actually made me cry. It's in this book (but you'll have to find it yourself).

This book is full of all the best jokes I know. Use them to find out which grown-ups are fun, and which ones are probably dead.

Or just tell them to your friends. I did!

PS Know a better one? Get it on the Awesome Map! See the back pages.

Let's Get Cracking!

What do you get if you cross a camel and a cow?
Lumpy milkshakes!

What's worse than getting your hair cut by a monkey?
A close shave with a gorilla!

 **Did you hear about the man who dreamed he was eating a marshmallow?**
When he woke up his pillow had disappeared.

What is the laziest vegetable?
A couch potato!

 **I'm so ugly.**
What can I do about it?
Hire yourself out for Halloween parties?

Who's there?
Honey bee.
Honey bee who?
Honey bee a dear and get me a lemonade.

What's the smallest ant in the world?

An infant!

I think I'm a moth.
Get out of the way, you're in my light!

What did the teddy bear say when he was offered second helpings?
No thanks, I'm stuffed.

Please can you help me? I'm lost. Will this path take me back to the main road?
No, you'll have to go by yourself!

What do you get if you cross a centipede and a parrot?
A walkie talkie!

Did you hear about the boy who was too poor to own a sled?
When it snowed he slid down the hills on his sister.

DOCTOR, DOCTOR!

I've turned into a window.
I see. Can you show me where the pane is?

What do campers need after breakfast?

A tea-pee!

I think I'm shrinking!
I'm sorry, I'm very busy. You'll just have to be a little patient.

DOCTOR, DOCTOR!

 **I'm turning into a piano!**
Just sit here while I make some notes.

What did Supremo the Escapologist never forget when he want on stage?
His amazing S-cape!

 **There's a dead fly in my coffee!**
Yes sir, it's the heat that kills them.

 **When I break wind it sounds like Taylor Swift!**
I see. And how long have you been having this gas-trick problem?

What's purple and five thousand miles long?

The Grape Wall of China

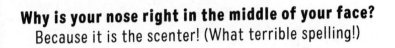

Why is your nose right in the middle of your face?
Because it is the scenter! (What terrible spelling!)

What do you get if you cross a duck with a firework?
A firequacker!

How do you make a hot dog?
Tell him the elevator is out of order!

Knock Knock!

Who's there?
Amish.
Amish who?
Awwww, how sweet.
I miss you too!

Why did Mozart get rid of his dogs?

He didn't like the sound of their Bach!

What do you call an underwater spy?
James Pond!

Knock Knock!

Who's there?
Foster.
Foster who?
Foster than a speeding bullet!

I've got pudding stuck in my ear!
Gjknkdfndhdhf fjdfnkn dfjdndkf...
**Sorry, what was that? You'll have
to speak up, I'm a trifle deaf.**

**Why did the stubborn little knight
miss his tea?**
Because he refused to
get down off his high horse.

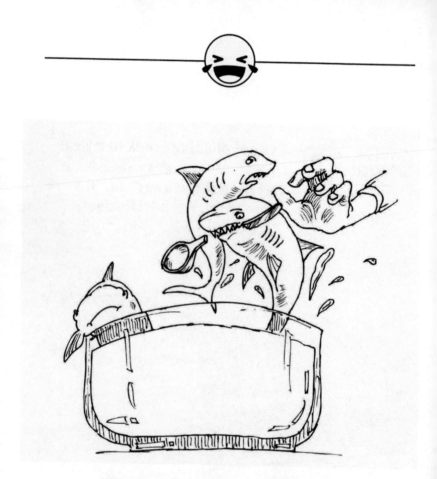

What's yellow and very dangerous?
Shark-infested custard.

Who's there?
Sultan.
Sultan who?
Sultan pepper!

 **I feel like a ladder!**
Right then, let's take this one
step at a time.

What did the cake say to the knife?

You wanna piece of me?

 **Who's there?**
Sweden.
Sweden who?
Sweden sour pork and some
prawn crackers, thanks for asking!

Where do rabbits go when they get married?
On bunny-moon!

 **Why was there thunder and
lightning in the laboratory?**
The scientists were brainstorming!

Who's there?
Eye-need-up.
Eye-need-up who?
Do you? The toilet's just up the stairs.

Why are ghosts cowards?

Because they don't have any guts.

What did one eye say to the other?
Between you and me, something smells!

Will I be able to play tennis when my arm is healed?
Absolutely.
Brilliant, I was terrible before.

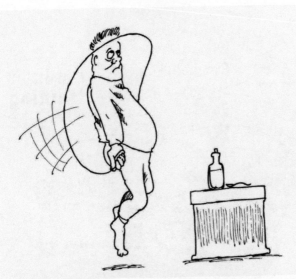

Why did the man jump up and down after taking his medicine?
He'd forgotten to shake the bottle!

Who's there?
Owls go.
Owls go who?
No, owls go whooooooooo....

What's a chicken's favourite drink?
Cocktails!

How do you weigh a whale?
At a whale-weigh station!

What do you get if you run over a budgie with a lawnmower?
Shredded tweet.

Why did the mathematician take a ruler to bed?
Because he wanted to see how long he would sleep!

Who's there?
Holly.
Holly who?
Hollydays are here again!

DOCTOR, DOCTOR! ✚

I've been to your surgery 87 times and I'm still sick. What do you suggest?
You could try these red pills.
Do they work?
Well nobody I've ever given them to has ever come back.

Why did the crab lose his job?

Because he couldn't stop pinching things!

How do you keep an idiot waiting?
I'll tell you later...

Who's there?
Winnie-thup.
Winnie-thup who?
You're right! It's
Winnie-the-Pooh!

**Why should you never invite
humming birds to your wedding?**
Because they never know the words!

**Why did Ellie throw the clock out
of the window?**
Because she wanted to see time fly!

Who's there?
Dewott.
Dewott who?
Dewott I say, I'm a police
officer!

What do you get when you plant kisses?
Two lips.

Who says oh, oh, oh?
Santa Claus walking backwards.

What direction do chickens swim?

Cluck-wise.

DOCTOR, DOCTOR! ✚

I think I am a bridge.
Why, what has come over you?
A car, two bikes and a lorry!

What do you call a cow that has run out of milk?
An udder failure.

 **Who's there?**
Spell.
Spell who?
W-H-O.
Well that was easy!

I saw Susie sitting in a shoe shine shop. Where she sits she shines, and where she shines she sits.

What did one star say to another?
Glad to meteor!

What is a pretzel's favourite dance?

The Twist!

How do you know when there's an elephant hiding under your bed?
You bump your head on the ceiling!

Where does a boat go when it's sick?
To the dock!

Who's there?
Hawaii.
Hawaii who?
I'm fine, Hawaii you?

Knock Knock!

Who's there?
Howard!
Howard who?
Howard I know?

A box of biscuits, a box of mixed biscuits and a biscuit mixer

TONGUE TWISTER

What are grizzlies called when they get caught in the rain?
Drizzly bears.

Why did the magician give up his Indian Rope Trick show?
Because he couldn't make ends meet.

Knock Knock!
Who's there?
Cereal.
Cereal who?
Cereal pleasure to meet you!

Where do Martians go to drink?

To a Mars bar!

Knock Knock!
Who's there?
Ada.
Ada who?
Ada burger for lunch!

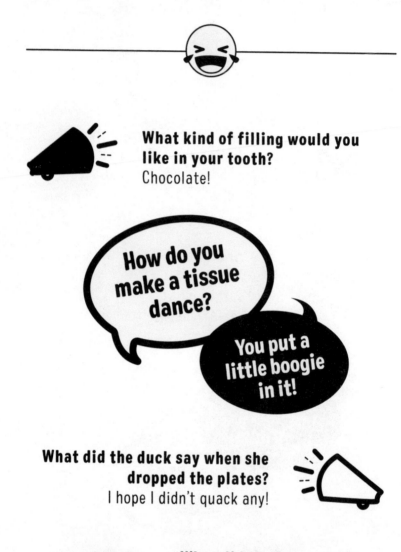

What kind of filling would you like in your tooth?
Chocolate!

How do you make a tissue dance?

You put a little boogie in it!

What did the duck say when she dropped the plates?
I hope I didn't quack any!

What did the boy octopus say to the girl octopus?
Can I hold your hand, hand, hand, hand, hand, hand, hand, hand?

Why do witches ride brooms?
Vacuum cleaners are too heavy.

Why was the clock sick?

It was run down.

**Why do mother kangaroos
hate rainy days?**
Because the children come inside to play!

What did the silly flower say to the bike?
My petals are prettier than yours.

What's faster, hot or cold?
Hot, because you can always
catch a cold.

Who's there?
Yukon.
Yukon who?
Yukon say that again!

Did you hear the joke about the strawberry jam? I'm not telling you. You might spread it!

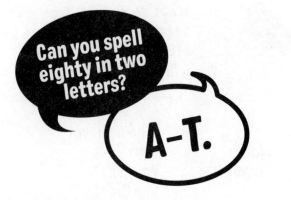

Can you spell eighty in two letters?

A-T.

What's big and ugly and arrives every morning to brighten your mum's day?
The school bus.

Do you serve crabs?
Certainly sir, we serve anybody.

What do you call a teacher with a bus on his shoulders?
Head coach.

What do you get from a dog who's been misbehaving in an artist's studio?
A lick of fresh paint!

Who's there?
Dan!
Dan who?
Dan Druff!

Why do monsters love busy trains?
Because they love going chew-chew!

Why does a flamingo lift up one leg?
Because if it lifted up both legs it would fall over!

Knock Knock!

Who's there?
Kenya.
Kenya who?
Kenya open the door, it's freezing!

What do you give train spotters for Christmas?
Platform shoes!

Knock Knock!

Who's there?
Voodoo.
Voodoo who?
Voodoo you think you are?

Where do pencils go for vacation?
Pencil-vania.

Why did the computer go to the doctor?

It had a virus.

This egg is disgusting!
I'm afraid I can't help, sir. I only lay the table.

Waiter, Waiter!

Which animal goes to sleep with its shoes on?
A horse!

What do you call a cross between a freckle and a spot?
A speckle.

What happens if an elephant sits in front of you at the cinema?
You'll miss the film.

Knock Knock!

Who's there?
Dishes.
Dishes who?
Dishes how I talk since I lost my teeth.

The teacher asked Simon if he could say his name backwards. "No mis," he replied. The teacher smiled and gave him extra play time. (Think about it!)

How do you make a fruit punch?
Give it boxing lessons.

 Who's there?
Snow.
Snow who?
Snow use. I forgot my name!

What did the judge say to the dentist?
Do you swear to pull the tooth, the whole tooth, and nothing but the tooth?

Why did the new music teacher get locked out of his classroom?
His keys were inside the piano!

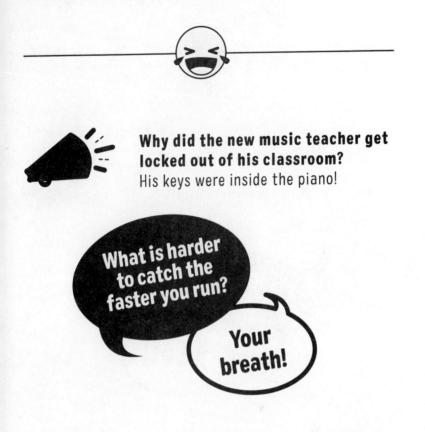

What is harder to catch the faster you run?

Your breath!

Pencils could be made with erasers on both ends, but what would be the point?

Dad, can you write in the dark?
I think so. What is it you want me to write?
Your signature on my report.

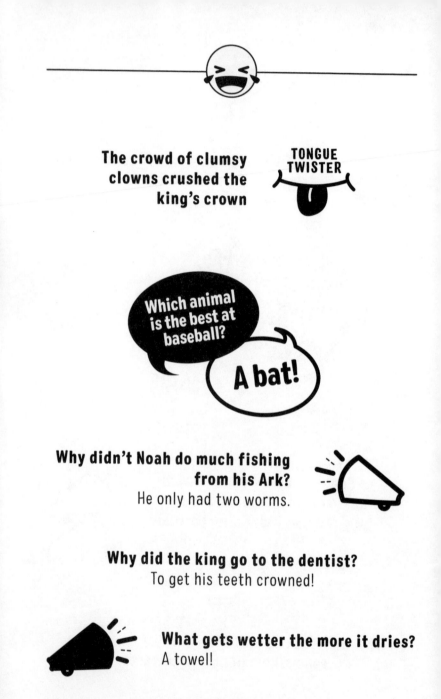

The crowd of clumsy clowns crushed the king's crown

TONGUE TWISTER

Which animal is the best at baseball?

A bat!

Why didn't Noah do much fishing from his Ark?
He only had two worms.

Why did the king go to the dentist?
To get his teeth crowned!

What gets wetter the more it dries?
A towel!

AWESOME JOKES THAT EVERY 8 YEAR OLD SHOULD KNOW!

Why did the boy never see any films at the cinema?
Because every time he went they tore his ticket in half!

What's the windiest board game?
Draughts!

How do you fix a broken robot?

With elbow grease!

Why are garbage collectors so miserable?
Because they're always down in the dumps.

Why did Santa book Rudolph in for a service?
Because his tail light was broken!

Welcome to the Clown Sleep Clinic, where we guarantee that all our patients will get forty winks.

What's the best luggage for a short holiday?

A briefcase!

How do you hire a horse?
Stand it on some bricks!

Why did the clumsy chef quit his job?
He kept getting egg on his face.

Twins went to the doctor for tests. The second one will need to come back because as everybody knows, you can't get blood out of a clone.

**Doctor, Doctor!
I think I'm a dog.**
How long have you felt like this?
Ever since I was a puppy!

**What did the balloon principal of the
balloon school say to the balloon boy when
he found a pin in the boy's pocket?**
You've let me down, you've let the school down,
but most of all you've let yourself down.

How does a florist lock up his shop?
Using a daisy chain!

Why did the girl throw the butter?
To see the butter fly.

Why do cows wear bells?
Because their horns don't work.

Why do tennis players make the best magicians?
Because they always have an ace up their sleeve.

What do you call a pile-up of clowns?
A happy accident!

Stanley opened a milkshake shop with over 10,000 flavours. But it went out of business because every customer who saw the menu went bananas.

What does a farmer do at the end of every month?
Claims his eggs-pences.

Why did the fishmonger get new gloves for Christmas?

Because he couldn't feel his fishfingers.

What's the first thing the little girl did on Christmas morning?
Flushed with excitement.

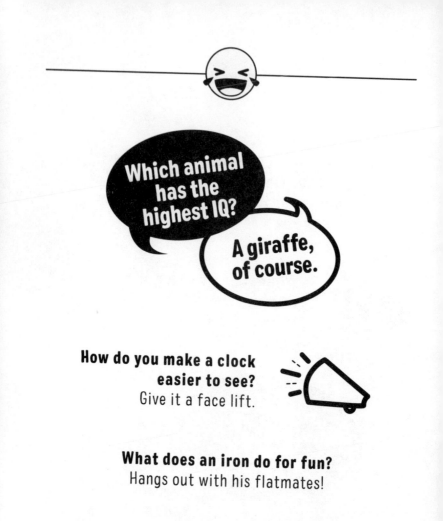

Which animal has the highest IQ?

A giraffe, of course.

How do you make a clock easier to see?
Give it a face lift.

What does an iron do for fun?
Hangs out with his flatmates!

What's the loudest section of Kermit's orchestra?
The froghorns!

Waiter, Waiter!

Bring me the bill.
How did you find your steak, sir?
It was hiding under the carrots.

Why did the village idiot hire a steamroller to drive over his potato patch?
He wanted to grow mashed potatoes!

When is the best time to go to the dentist?
Tooth-hurty.

When is the second-best time to go to the dentist?
Tooth-hurty too.

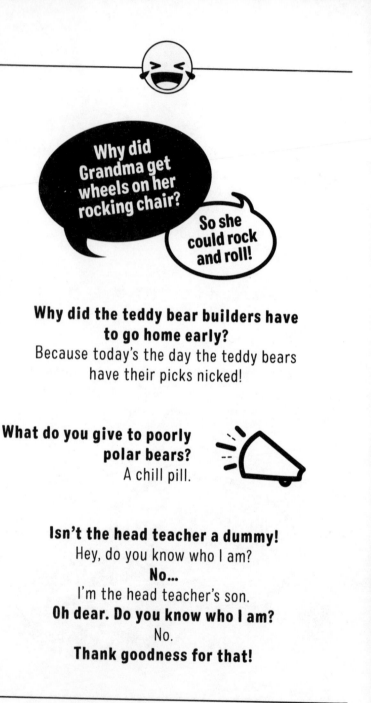

Why did Grandma get wheels on her rocking chair?

So she could rock and roll!

Why did the teddy bear builders have to go home early?
Because today's the day the teddy bears have their picks nicked!

What do you give to poorly polar bears?
A chill pill.

Isn't the head teacher a dummy!
Hey, do you know who I am?
No...
I'm the head teacher's son.
Oh dear. Do you know who I am?
No.
Thank goodness for that!

What did you learn in school today?
Not enough apparently, I have to go back tomorrow!

Why are leopards so bad at playing hide and seek?
Because they're always spotted!

What's the fastest way for bugs to get across town?
Take the flyover!

When do vets get busy?
When it's raining cats and dogs.

What do librarians take with them when they go fishing?
Bookworms.

Teacher: What do you get when you mix the chemicals Ba and Na^2?
Pupil: A banana?

Who's there?
Sis!
Sis who?
Sis any way to keep a friend waiting?

How did the Dad banana spoil the baby banana?
He left him out in the sun too long.

What is Thor's favourite food?
Thor-tillas.

Why was the birthday cake so hard?
It was a marble cake.

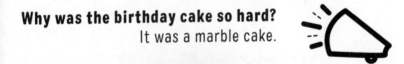

What is a bunny's favourite game?

Hopscotch!

What do you call chilly cows?

Friesian!

Where do space farmers grow their carrots?
In force fields.

How do police catch a wig thief?
They carefully comb the area.

What do you call people who like shopping for fancy dresses?
Frill seekers.

 **What do you call someone trying to buy a high wire?**
A tension-seeker!

Why did the ballroom dancer cancel the show?
He'd come down with the foxtrots!

What's the noisiest type of fair?
A fanfare!

What does a baby computer call its dad?

Data!

What do you get when you cross a bear with a honey jar?
A very sticky situation!

Why do French people eat snails?
Because they don't like fast food!

Who's there?
Leia.
Leia who?
Leia hand on me and I'll have you arrested!

Do you call this a three-course meal?
Of course, of course, of course!

Why did the teacher wear sunglasses?
Because her pupils were so bright!

Help! I've only got 59 seconds to live!
I'll be with you in a minute.

What did the lawyer name his first daughter?
Sue!

If a seagull flies over the sea, what do you call a bird that flies over the bay?
A bagel!

Who's there?
Alaska!
Alaska who?
Alaska friend if she's got the key!

How did they arrest the tomato thief?
The police caught him red handed.

When is a door not a door?

When it's ajar!

What's a teddy bear's favourite pasta?
Taglia-teddy!

Waiter, Waiter! There's a worm on my plate.
That's your sausage, sir.

What do you call someone who's very good looking but not a nice person to know?
Pretty ugly.

What goes stamp stamp stamp donk?

A horse with a wooden leg.

Why did the musician get fired?
For fiddling his expenses.

 **I'm really worried about my breathing.**
I'll soon put a stop to that!

What do lawyers wear to court?

Lawsuits!

What school do surfers go to?
A boarding school!

Who invented fire?
Some bright spark.

What is the highest digit?
An astro-naught!

My Mum has gone to a mirror shop. She called Dad to say she can see herself staying all day.

Why do you drive down a parkway, but park in a driveway? Answer that, smartypants.

What's the difference between roast beef and pea soup?
You can roast beef, but you can't pea soup!

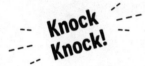
Who's there?
Johnny DingleDangle.
Johnny DingleDangle who?
How many other Johnny DingleDangles do you know? Let me in!

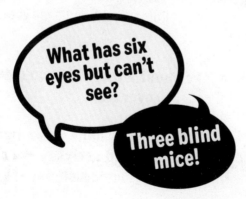

Why did the vampire retrain as a nurse?

It was in his blood.

Why didn't the sun go to college?
Because it already had thousands of degrees!

Knock Knock!
Who's there?
Robin.
Robin who?
Robin you! Hand over your wallet!

I'd tell you a joke about a wall, but you'd never get over it.

Why do cockerels get up so early?
They set their alarm cluck.

**If slow old men use walking sticks,
what do fast old men use?**
Hurry-canes!

Who's there?
Amanda.
Amanda who?
**Amanda fix your broken
window.**

**What would you like to be when you
grow up, son?**
A garbage collector.
Really? Why?
Because they only work on Mondays!

What do you call a noodle that's not welcome?

An impaster!

Why were the ancient Egyptian children confused?
Because their daddies were mummies!

What did daddy potato say to baby potato?
Hurry up, small fry!

Knock Knock!

Who's there?
Dewey.
Dewey who?
Dewey really have to turn this into a joke?

If a black bug bleeds black blood, what colour blood does a blue bug bleed?

TONGUE TWISTER

What type of lights did Noah fit to his Ark?
Floodlights!

Why do golfers wear two pairs of pants?
In case they get a hole in one!

 **Why did Tom let his sister borrow the ice skates first?**
To find out if the ice was thick enough!

What's grey, has four legs and a huge trunk?
A mouse going on a long vacation.

Barber, your hands are filthy!
Yes, I'm sorry about that. Nobody has asked for a shampoo yet.

**What do pigs give to each other
on Valentine's Day?**
Kisses and hogs.

Who's there?
It's Norma Lee.
Norma Lee who?
It's Norma Lee easy for me to
open this door, but it's stuck!

Why did the toilet roll head down the hill?
To get to the bottom.

Growing grey goats graze
great green grassy groves.

 **What kind of teacher doesn't break wind in public?**
A private tooter.

What did the fish say to the cloud?

High! (Geddit?!)

Why did the skeleton go to the barbecue?
He'd heard about the spare ribs.

 **TONGUE TWISTER** **The peppy puppy the prince presented to the princess produced piles of poop in the palace.**

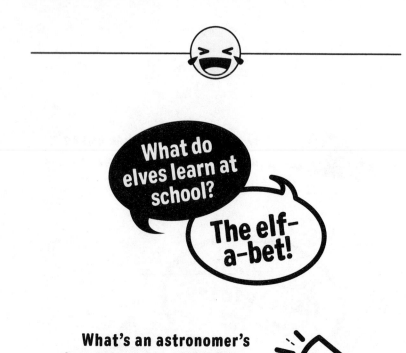

What do elves learn at school?

The elf-a-bet!

What's an astronomer's favourite type of window?
A skylight.

What goes in pink and comes out blue?
A swimmer in a cold lake!

Why is the letter T like an island?
Because it's in the middle of 'water'.

When were there only three vowels in the alphabet?
Long ago, before U and I were born.

What's the difference between a supermarket and a lion enclosure?
If you don't know, I'm never sending you to get the groceries.

What's the difference between a storm and a poorly lion?
One pours with rain, the other roars with pain!

Who's there?
Hammond.
Hammond who?
Hammond eggs, please, with extra fries!

Which meal comes with free buttons?

A jacket potato!

Knock Knock!

Who's there?
Arthur.
Arthur who?
Arthur any sandwiches left? I'm starving!

Where do they make satis?

In a satisfactory!

A man in a cinema notices a badger sitting next to him. "Are you a badger?" he asks, surprised. The badger nodded. "What are you doing at the movies?" "Well, I liked the book," said the badger.

Why did Johnny use the password MickeyMinnieOlafElsa **for the Disney website?**
Because it told him to use 4 characters!

**Doctor, Doctor! I've got terrible wind!
What can you give me for it?**
How about a kite?

Dad, I'm stuck up this tree!
Well why don't you come down the
same way you came up?
But I came up head first!

Where do all the trendy mice live?
In their mousepads.

What are the strongest days of the week?
Saturday and Sunday, because the others are week days!

Which is the hottest letter of the alphabet?
B, because it makes oil boil. (It's a head-scratcher!)

What type of tree grows fingers?
A palm tree!

Why do stunt pilots often forget to put their pants on?
Because they've always got their head in the clouds.

What does a man with two left feet wear?

Flip-flips!

Why did the little boy oil his mice?
Because they kept squeaking!

What has a bottom at the top?
Your leg!

Please, miss! How do you spell ichael?
Don't you mean Michael?
No. I've written the M already.

What do you call a bottom with a gun?

A crack commando!

Why did the dim burglar crash through the window?
He forgot to let go of the brick.

I had to get rid of my builder. Every time I asked him to do something he hit the roof.

Why are you late for school?
Because of the sign just down the road.
What sign?
The one that says "School Ahead. Slow!"

What kind of plates do they use on Mars?
Flying saucers!

What's round and a bit of a bully?
A vicious circle.

Have you heard about the old man who lost his wallet in his bedroom, but looked for it in the garden?
He said the light was better outside.

What goes ha-ha-ha-bonk?

A man laughing his head off!

Where's the best place to eat dinner on a long journey?
At a fork in the road.

What does a ball do when it rolls to the bottom of the hill?
Looks round.

What do you get if you cross a cat with an octagon?
An octopus!

What do you get if you cross a fish and two elephants?
Swimming trunks.

Why did the village idiot look into the mirror with his eyes shut?
He wanted to find out what he looked like when he was asleep!

What's the difference between a baker and an elephant?
One bakes the bread, the other breaks the bed.

What's the safest way to hammer nails into wood?
Get your brother to hold the nails.

Where's the best place to go on a ship?

Where the funnel be!

I had my first lesson at the Art College for Idiots today. They asked me to draw a pair of curtains.

Why shouldn't you put the letter M into the freezer?
Because it turns ice into mice.

If you have 6 apples in one hand and 9 in the other, what have you got?
Huge hands!

Why is a highway your best friend?
Because it always has a shoulder to cry on!

Why did the sign fall off the old-fashioned sweet shop?
Because the owner had fudged it!

What do you get when you cross a PC with an elephant?
Lots of memory!

What kind of cereal do Harry Potter fans eat?

Huffle Puffs!

Why did the village idiot put razor blades in his potato patch?
Because he was trying to grow chips!

Why is a squirrel coat the best at keeping out water?
Well you've never seen a squirrel with an umbrella, have you?

What's a pirate's favourite country?

AAARRRGH-entina!

Why did the film critic storm out of the car showroom?
Because there were too many spoilers!

What did the car say to the wheel?
I'm tired of you giving me the run around!

What did the duck detective say to his partner?
I hope we can quack this case.

Which athlete finds it easy to keep warm in winter?
A long jumper.

Knock Knock!

Who's there?
Eskimo!
Eskimo who?
Eskimo questions,
I'll tell you no lies.

Oi! You, boy! Stop throwing stones! You nearly broke my window!
I'm sorry. Would you like me to try again?

Why are toilet paper jokes really weak?
Because it's tear-rible!

Why are giraffes so slow to say sorry?
It takes them a long time to swallow their pride.

What do you call a sleeping bull?
A bulldozer!

Waiter, Waiter!

I'll have the pie, please.
Anything with it, sir?
If it's like last time you'd better bring me a drill and a saw.

 'Sticks and stones may break my bones but words will never hurt me,' said the wise old man. But then someone hit him with a dictionary.

If money doesn't grow on trees, why do banks have branches?

 **Who's there?**
Zaire.
Zaire who?
Zaire air is so polluted round here!

What do ghosts like on their dessert?

Whipped scream!

Knock Knock!

Who's there?
Ice cream soda!
Ice cream soda who?
Ice cream soda whole
neighbourhood will hear.

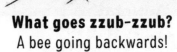

What goes zzub-zzub?
A bee going backwards!

**Where do you find information
about eggs?**
In the hen-cyclopedia!

I keep getting into fights.
Hmm. And how long have you had this complaint?
Ask me that again and I'll knock your block off.

What did the traffic light say to the car?
Can you look away? I'm changing.

How do you know if it's cold outside?
When you milk a brown cow you get chocolate ice cream.

Why did the termite eat a sofa and two chairs?
It had a suite tooth.

Knock Knock!
Who's there?
Yacht.
Yacht who?
Yacht to know me by now!

Knock Knock!

Who's there?
Weevil.
Weevil who?
Weevil, weevil rock you!

Why did the maths book look so sad?

Because it had so many problems!

What did the triangle say to the circle?
You're pointless!

What do you get if you cross some ants with some tics?
Lots of silly antics.

Who's there?
Thermos.
Thermos who?
Thermos be a better 'Knock Knock' joke than this.

Why was the robot mad?
People kept pushing his buttons.

**Why did the salad
win the race?**
Because the spaghetti couldn't get pasta!

What do they teach in witching school?

Spelling!

Why did the man run around his bed?
Because he was trying to catch up on his sleep!

What do you call a polar bear on thin ice?
An ice breaker.

What do you call a Frenchman in sandals?
Philippe Feloppe.

TONGUE TWISTER

I have got a date at a quarter to eight; I'll see you at the gate, so don't be late.

A mother was preparing pancakes for her sons, Jake and Alfie. They started to fight about who would get the first pancake.

"If Jesus were sitting here," said their mother, "he would let his brother have the first pancake. He'd wait."

Jake looked at his brother. "Alfie, you be Jesus."

Who's there?
Sherlock.
Sherlock who?
Sherlock your door tonight, there are burglars around.

How does the man in the moon cut his hair?

Eclipse it!

What goes up and never comes down?

Your age!

A skunk sat on a stump and thunk the stump stunk, but the stump thunk the skunk stunk.

TONGUE TWISTER

What did the polar bear eat after the dentist filled its tooth?
The dentist!

What do you call a car squashed by a dinosaur?
Tyrannosaurus wreck!

What is a horse's favourite sport?
Stable tennis!

Who's there?
Adair.
Adair who?
Adair once, but now I'm as bald as an egg.

Why don't cannibals eat clowns?

They taste funny!

I keep thinking I'm a vampire.
Necks, please!

Why does Peter Pan fly?
Because he neverlands.

Why is England the wettest country?
Because the queen has reigned for years.

Knock Knock!

Who's there?
Lionel!
Lionel who?
Lionel bite you if you get too close!

What do you call a very rude bird?

A mockingbird!

What sits at the bottom of the ocean and shakes?
A nervous wreck!

Waiter, Waiter!

Do you have frogs' legs?
No sir, I've always walked like this.

What do you call a dinosaur with an extensive vocabulary?
A thesaurus.

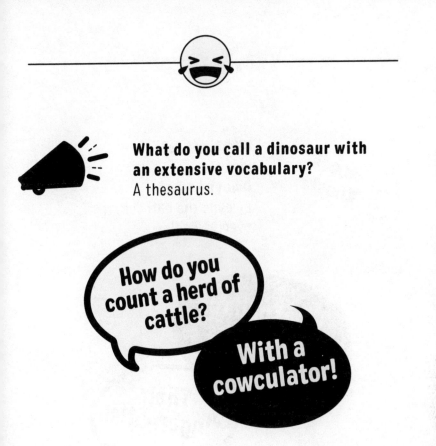

How do you count a herd of cattle?

With a cowculator!

My dog has just swallowed a dictionary.
I expect he'll have a few words in the garden tomorrow.

Knock Knock!

Who's there?
Nana.
Nana who?
Nana your business.

Who's there?
Dwayne.
Dwayne who?
Dwayne the bathtub, it's overflowing!

What nails do carpenters hate to hit?

Their fingernails!

Waiter, Waiter!

Bring me soup with a hair in it, some cold greasy fries and some undercooked chicken.
We don't do food like that, sir!
What's changed? You did yesterday!

What do you call a bruise on a T-Rex?

A dino-sore!

Knock Knock!

Who's there?
Oink oink!
Oink oink who?
Make up your mind... Are you a pig or an owl?

Did you hear about the hundred hares that escaped from the field?
The police had to comb the area.

There were ten cats in a hot air balloon and one jumped out. How many were left?
None: they were copycats!

What is a knight's favourite fish?

Swordfish!

What did the baby Egyptian say when he got lost?
I want my mummy! (Did you guess that?)

What do you call a cow with a nervous twitch?
Beef jerky.

What do you call a dinosaur that never gives up?
A try- try- try-ceratops!

 **I feel like a large bank note.**
Go shopping, the change will do you good.

Why was the weatherman's head wet?
Because he had a brainstorm.

What do Winnie the Pooh and Bozo the Clown have in common?
The same middle name, silly.

Who's there?
Razor!
Razor who?
Razor hands, this is a stick up!

When I grow up I want to be a bus driver.

Well I won't stand in your way.

 **Who's there?**
Doughnut.
Doughnut who?
Doughnut ask,
it's top secret.

What do planets
like to read?

Comet
books!

 **I keep stealing things when
I go shopping. What can you
give me for it?**
Try this medicine... and if it
doesn't work come back and bring
me a new smartphone.

Why did the dinosaur cross the road?
The chicken hadn't evolved yet.

Change is hard. Have you ever tried to bend a coin?

Why did the man lose his job at the orange juice factory?
He couldn't concentrate!

I can't get to sleep.
Sit on the edge of the bed.
You'll soon drop off.

Why do we cook bacon, but bake cookies?

Who's there?
Norway.
Norway who?
Norway am I telling you any
more of my jokes.

Now it's your turn!

Here are some awesome jokes sent in by 8-year-olds from around the world. Can you do better? See page 97!

What is a cheerleader's favourite food?
Cheerios!
(From Alex, Washington)

SENT IN BY BEN, 8, FROM ISLE OF WIGHT

playing for milk money

What do you call a cow in a band?
A moo-sician!

Knock Knock!

Who's there?
Europe.
Europe who?
You're a poo too!
(From Archie, Lincoln)

What did the slug say to the shy snail?
Why don't you come out of your shell?
(From Millie, Oxford)

What's the sea's favourite football team?
Shell-sea United!
(From Charlie, Birmingham)

Knock Knock!

Who's there?
Robin.
Robin who?
I'm Robin Banks!
(From Oliver, 8, Tunbridge Wells)

What does a duck eat with his soup?
Quackers.
(From Amy, Perth)

Mix and match!

Can you match each joke to its punchline? But watch out: there are two questions missing! You'll find them in **More Awesome Jokes Every 8 Year Old Should Know** – buy it now!

Which pet needs cleaning but not feeding?

Which food shines at night?

Where's the best place to make bread?

What's the loudest sound at a birdwatchers' picnic?

What makes a robot so attractive?

How do you make a sandcastle out of ice cream?

What's the wrong way to hold your pen?

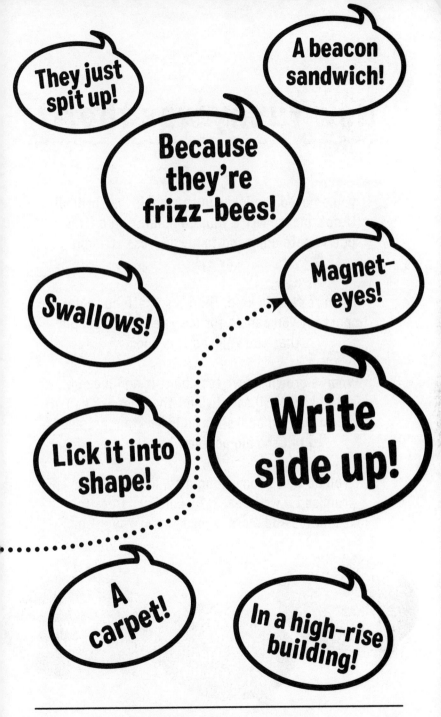

How funny was that?

If you enjoyed the jokes in this book, I'm thrilled! (If not, please write your complaint on a fifty pound note and send to my address straight away).

If you're feeling kind, there's something really important you can do for me – tell other people that you enjoyed this book.

When a grown-up writes about it on Amazon, more people will see it... and that means I can carry on writing books for children. You just need to tell the big people what to say!

If you do write something nice, let me know – I promise I'll write back. My email address for jokes, notes and more is jokes@matwaugh.co.uk

Mat

I know a great joke!

Send me your best joke and I'll put it on my **World Map of Awesome Jokes**!

Head over to the map now to discover silly jokes, clever jokes and weird jokes. Some jokes rhyme, some are a crime, but they're all sent in by children like you!

Will you be the first on the map from your town?

Put your awesome joke here at
www.matwaugh.co.uk/jokemap

About Mat Waugh

It's funny what makes you laugh, isn't it? Sometimes it's a great joke, and I hope you found a few in this book. Sometimes you don't even need words. It could be a funny look from a friend in class. Or maybe it's something that wasn't supposed to happen.

Once, when I was about your age, I was in the back of my aunt's car on a Christmas Day. The sun reflected brightly in the deep puddles from the night's rain.

My aunt wasn't very good at driving. As we approached a dip in the road we could see a vicar cycling towards us, on his way to church. Dad told my aunt to slow down... but she pressed the wrong pedal. The car hit the water with a mighty SPLOOSH! I looked back to see a huge wave swamping the vicar and his bike. He shook his fists at us, but my aunt didn't even notice. I'm still laughing... but I bet the vicar isn't.

I have three daughters to make me laugh now. (Not all the time though: they drive me bananas.)

I live in Tunbridge Wells, which is a lively, lovely town in the south east of England. It's not a very funny place, mind you..

I've always written a lot. I've done lots of writing for other people – mostly serious stuff – but now I write silly, crazy and funny books as well.

Talking of crazy, I had a mad year when I thought I wanted to be a teacher. But then I found out how hard teachers work and that you have to buy your own biscuits. So now I just visit schools to eat their snacks and talk to children about stories.

Last thing: I love hearing from readers. Thoughts, jokes... anything. If that's you, then get in touch.

✉ mail@matwaugh.co.uk
www.matwaugh.co.uk

Or, if you're old enough:

facebook.com/matwaughauthor
twitter.com/matwaugh

Three more to try!

Cheeky Charlie vol 1-6
Meet Harriet and her small, stinky brother. Together, they're trouble. Fabulously funny stories for kids aged 6 and up.

Fantastic Wordsearches
Wordsearch with a difference: themed, crossword clues and hidden words await!

The Fun Factor
When the fun starts vanishing, it seems Thora is the only one to notice. The headmaster is definitely up to no good, but what about Dad's new girlfriend? A mystery adventure for gadget-loving kids aged 8 and up.

Available from Amazon and local bookshops.

MORE AWESOME JOKES FOR 8 YEAR OLDS OUT NOW!

Be the first to know about new stuff! Sign up for my emails at matwaugh.co.uk